The Cashflow Accelerator Method

How to Use Your Income and Home Equity to Destroy Debt Years Faster Without Refinancing or New Loans

By Joseph G. C

Licensed Mortgage Broker,

Copyright & Legal Notice

Published by Live Stronger Faster

First Edition, 2026

Table of Contents

Forward

Most people are trapped in debt not because they don't earn enough money, but because they were taught the wrong system for managing it. They were told to send payments once a month, carry balances, wait years for principal to shrink, and hope that eventually their mortgage, credit cards, and personal loans would somehow disappear on their own. In reality, that traditional model was never designed to make you debt-free quickly. It was designed to keep you paying interest for as long as possible. What this book introduces is a completely different way of thinking about money, cash flow, and home equity. It is not about taking on more debt, gambling with your house, or making risky financial moves. It is about learning how to move money through your life in a smarter, more intentional way so that every dollar works harder and attacks your balances instead of feeding the banks.

This book exists because thousands of homeowners already have the tools they need to wipe out debt sitting quietly inside their financial structure, but no one ever shows them how to use those tools properly. You earn income. You pay bills. You likely have home equity. You probably have high-interest debts. The problem is not that these elements exist, but that they are disconnected and poorly coordinated. When income flows into checking accounts and then trickles out slowly through monthly payments, interest has time to grow. When equity sits unused, it does nothing to reduce that interest. The Cashflow Accelerator Method brings these pieces together into a single system, where income, expenses, and equity are synchronized in a way that collapses interest and forces balances down far faster than traditional payment plans ever could.

As a licensed mortgage broker who has spent years analyzing how debt truly behaves inside real households, I have seen one pattern repeat over and over. Two families can have the same income, the same mortgage, and the same debts, yet one stays in debt for thirty years while the other becomes debt-free in a fraction of the time. The difference is not discipline or sacrifice. It is structure. The way money moves through your accounts matters more than how much you make. This book teaches you how to restructure that flow so that debt is constantly under pressure instead of comfortably growing in the background. When you understand how to move cash strategically, you can attack interest daily rather than monthly, and that alone changes everything.

Most people believe debt only shrinks when they send a payment. That belief is one of the biggest financial myths in modern money. In reality, debt shrinks whenever your balance is lower, even for a single day. Interest is calculated daily, and it is always working against you unless you deliberately disrupt it. This book shows you how to use your income and equity as tools that temporarily suppress balances, even if that money needs to be used again later. When balances are lower, interest has less to feed on. Over time, that reduction compounds in your favor instead of the bank's. You are not paying more money. You are changing how long the money sits against the debt.

What makes this system so powerful is that it does not require refinancing, new loans, or risky financial products. It uses what you already have. Your paycheck. Your expenses. Your home equity line. Your existing debts. The difference is that instead of letting money drift passively through your accounts, you direct it with precision. The goal is not to borrow more, but to use short-term access to capital to create long-term interest destruction. This book will walk you through how to think like a financial engineer rather than a bill payer. When you do, the entire debt landscape changes.

This method also restores something that most people have lost in the modern financial system, which is control. Traditional debt management puts you at the mercy of lenders, schedules, and amortization tables you never designed. You simply follow instructions and hope for the best.

The Cashflow Accelerator Method puts you back in the driver's seat. You decide when balances drop. You decide when money moves. You decide how aggressively debt is attacked. Instead of waiting for years to pass, you actively compress time by forcing interest to starve. That is what creates the dramatic payoff speed this system is known for.

This book is especially powerful when combined with everything you have learned in the previous volumes of The Home Equity Wealth Series. You already understand how HELOCs work, how to qualify, how to manage risk, and how to access equity responsibly. Now you are learning how to weaponize that knowledge for one of the most important financial victories possible: total debt freedom. This is not about using equity recklessly. It is about using it intelligently, temporarily, and strategically so that it multiplies the power of your income instead of increasing your long-term liabilities.

By the time you finish this book, you will no longer look at your mortgage, your credit cards, or your bank account the same way. You will understand how money flows, how interest feeds, and how to shut it down. You will see how homeowners quietly eliminate decades of debt without changing their lifestyle, simply by changing the sequence and timing of their money. That is the real secret. Not earning more, not budgeting harder, but moving money smarter. This final book in the Home Equity Wealth Series is the bridge between knowledge and true financial freedom, because once your debt is gone, your income finally becomes yours.

Chapter 1

The Hidden Mechanics of Debt and Cash Flow

Debt is not defeated by how much you pay, but by how long money sits against what you owe. Every loan in the world, whether it is a mortgage, credit card, auto loan, or personal line of credit, calculates interest based on the balance that exists each day. When a balance is high, interest grows. When a balance is low, interest shrinks. The problem is that most people only interact with their debt once per month, when they send a payment. For the other twenty-nine or thirty days, the bank is quietly charging interest on the full balance as if nothing ever changed. This creates the illusion that you are making progress, while in reality most of what you send is simply paying for time, not reducing what you owe. When you understand this, you begin to see that debt is not controlled by payments, but by daily balance exposure.

Cash flow is the true weapon against debt. Cash flow is not how much you earn in a year, but how money moves through your accounts in real time. When income comes in and sits in a checking account while bills wait to be paid, that money is not working for you. At the same time, your debts are sitting at full balance accumulating interest. The Cashflow Accelerator

Method changes this relationship by redirecting income immediately to suppress debt balances the moment money arrives. Even if that money needs to be used again later for expenses, the temporary reduction in balance still destroys interest that would have otherwise been charged. Over time, those tiny daily savings compound into massive reductions in total interest paid.

Home equity plays a unique role in this system because it gives you access to large amounts of low-interest, revolving capital that can be used strategically without locking you into new long-term loans. A home equity line of credit is not meant to replace your mortgage or become a new permanent balance. Instead, it acts as a financial buffer and control valve. When used correctly, it allows you to move money in and out in a way that keeps your highest-interest debts constantly suppressed. You are not adding debt, you are temporarily repositioning it so that interest is minimized while principal is attacked.

What makes this system powerful is the difference between static debt and dynamic debt. Static debt is what most people have. A fixed balance, a fixed payment, and a fixed schedule that barely changes from month to month. Dynamic debt is when balances are constantly being pushed down by incoming cash flow, even if they rise again later when expenses are paid.

The net effect is that the average balance across the month becomes far lower than it would be under a normal payment system. Since interest is calculated on average daily balance, this creates a permanent advantage in your favor.

The real breakthrough comes when you realize that you do not need to permanently pay off a balance to benefit from lowering it. Even a temporary reduction saves interest. If a credit card sits at $20,000 for thirty days, you pay interest on $20,000 for thirty days. If your income flows in and knocks that balance down to $5,000 for ten days before bills are paid, you only pay interest on $20,000 for twenty days and $5,000 for ten days. That alone dramatically changes how fast the debt shrinks. The Cashflow Accelerator Method simply repeats this process over and over, using income and equity to create frequent, deep balance reductions.

Traditional budgeting focuses on restricting spending. This system focuses on optimizing timing. You still pay your bills. You still live your life. But instead of letting money sit idle, you force it to neutralize debt first. Every dollar becomes a temporary debt-destroying tool before it is ever used for groceries, utilities, or entertainment. This is why people using this system often eliminate decades of interest without increasing their income or sacrificing their lifestyle. By the end of this chapter, you should understand one core truth: debt is a time problem, not just a money problem. When you shorten the time that balances remain high, you collapse the total interest that can be charged. The rest of this book will show you how to build that time-destroying machine using the money you already earn and the equity you already have.

Practical Example: *How Cash Flow Collapses Interest Using Real Numbers*

Let's look at a homeowner with a $300,000 mortgage at 6 percent interest and $25,000 in credit card debt at 18 percent interest. Their monthly income is $8,000. Their total monthly expenses including the mortgage, cards, and living costs are $6,000, leaving $2,000 in surplus cash flow. Under the traditional system, this person sends $2,000 toward their credit cards every month. The bank calculates interest on the full $25,000 balance every single day until the payment arrives, then repeats the process the next month. At 18 percent, that $25,000 generates about $375 in interest per month. Even after paying $2,000, only about $1,625 actually reduces the balance, and the next month interest starts all over again.

Now imagine this homeowner has a $100,000 home equity line of credit at 8 percent. Instead of sending $2,000 to the credit cards once per month, they first use the HELOC to pay the $25,000 credit card balance down to zero. Now the

$25,000 sits on the HELOC instead. The interest drops immediately because 8 percent is far lower than 18 percent. But the real magic comes from what happens next. When their $8,000 paycheck arrives, instead of sitting in checking, it is immediately deposited into the HELOC, reducing the balance from $25,000 down to $17,000. That means for however long that money stays there, interest is being calculated on $17,000 instead of $25,000.

Over the next thirty days, the homeowner pays their $6,000 in expenses out of the HELOC. As those bills are paid, the balance slowly rises back up. But here is the key: for many days or weeks, the balance is far lower than $25,000. Instead of paying interest on $25,000 for the entire month, they might pay interest on an average balance of $12,000. At 8 percent, $12,000 generates only about $80 in monthly interest instead of $375. That is a savings of $295 in one single month, without earning an extra dollar.

Now let's look at how this accelerates payoff. That $295 that was not paid in interest effectively becomes extra principal reduction. Add that to their $2,000 monthly surplus, and now they are paying off roughly $2,295 per month instead of $2,000. Over a year, that is an extra $3,540 in principal wiped out just from interest collapse. As the balance gets smaller, the effect compounds even more because less and less interest is being charged each month. The same process applies to the mortgage. Let's say the mortgage balance is $300,000. The homeowner uses the HELOC to temporarily drop the mortgage balance by $50,000 for part of the month. Even if that money has to be used again later, those days where the mortgage sits at $250,000 instead of $300,000 reduce interest permanently. At 6 percent, $50,000 avoided for ten days saves about $82 in interest. Do that every month and you save nearly $1,000 per year just by moving money at the right time.

When you add these two systems together, the effect multiplies. The credit cards disappear first because they have the highest interest. Once they are gone, the same cash flow attacks the HELOC. Once the HELOC is gone, the full cash flow attacks the mortgage. The homeowner did not increase their income. They did not refinance. They did not add risk. They simply used timing and flow to starve interest and redirect it into principal.

That is why this system works so powerfully. It does not rely on motivation, sacrifice, or luck. It relies on math. Lower balances mean lower interest. Lower interest means faster payoff. Faster payoff means financial freedom years earlier than most people ever imagine.

Chapter 2

Designing Your Personal Cashflow Engine

The Cashflow Accelerator Method only works when your accounts are structured correctly, because the system is not about chasing debt manually but about letting money automatically flow in a way that forces balances down. Most households are set up in a way that accidentally protects their debt instead of attacking it. Income flows into checking, bills are paid out over the month, and debts sit at full balance collecting interest every day. To reverse this, you must design a simple but powerful structure where every dollar you earn passes through a control point before it is allowed to be spent. That control point is the revolving equity account. When your income hits that account first, it immediately reduces your largest balance, which immediately reduces the amount of interest being charged. The longer money sits there, the more interest it destroys.

The first rule of this system is that your income must never idle. Idle money is wasted opportunity because while it sits in a checking account earning nothing, your debts are charging you interest. By routing all income into the revolving equity account, you create a financial gravity well where debt is constantly being pulled down. Checking accounts should no longer hold savings. They should only be used as pass-through accounts for expenses. The equity account becomes your true operating account, even though it technically is a loan. That sounds counterintuitive at first, but mathematically it makes sense because every dollar sitting there is reducing interest instead of earning a trivial amount in a savings account.

The second rule is that all expenses are paid out of the revolving equity account, not out of your paycheck. This is what allows your income to remain applied against your debt for as long as possible. When a paycheck arrives, it pushes the balance down. When you buy groceries, pay utilities, or cover your mortgage, the balance rises again. What matters is not that it rises, but how long it stays low. The longer it stays low, the more interest is erased. Over time, this creates a permanently shrinking average balance even if your lifestyle stays exactly the same.

The third rule is that surplus cash flow must never sit in checking or savings. If you earn more than you spend, that difference should remain inside the equity account where it permanently reduces the principal. That is how the system locks in progress. Even if balances fluctuate during the month, the long-term trend is always downward because every extra dollar remains buried inside the debt, starving it of interest.

The fourth rule is sequencing. High-interest debts should always be absorbed first. Credit cards, personal loans, and auto loans are transferred into the revolving equity account so that they immediately begin benefiting from the cashflow compression effect. Once those balances are gone, the same engine is pointed at the mortgage. This creates a cascading payoff effect where each debt disappears faster than the last, because the amount of cashflow attacking it keeps growing.

The fifth rule is discipline through automation. This system works best when income is direct-deposited into the equity account and bills are paid automatically from it. This removes emotion and decision-making from the process. The system becomes mechanical. Money comes in, balances drop. Money goes out, balances rise. But over time, the drop always exceeds the rise. That is how debt is defeated.

By building this structure, you are not just paying debt. You are engineering a cashflow engine. You are turning your income into a weapon that is always pointed at your balances, not just once a month, but every single day. That is what creates exponential progress instead of slow, linear payoff.

Practical Example: *Building a Real Cashflow Engine with Numbers*

Let's look at a household that earns $9,000 per month. Their mortgage is $2,400. Their credit cards total $18,000 at 19 percent. Their other living expenses are $4,600. That leaves $2,000 per month in surplus cash flow. They also have a $60,000 home equity line of credit at 8 percent.

First, they use the HELOC to pay off the $18,000 in credit cards. Now the credit cards are zero, and the HELOC balance becomes $18,000. Instead of paying 19 percent on $18,000, they are now paying 8 percent. That alone cuts the interest from about $285 per month down to about $120.

Next, their $9,000 paycheck is deposited into the HELOC. That immediately reduces the balance from $18,000 to $9,000. For however long that money remains there, interest is calculated on $9,000 instead of $18,000. If it stays there for even ten days, the interest savings are significant. At 8 percent, $18,000 generates about $120 per month, or about $4 per day. $9,000 generates about $60 per month, or about $2 per day. Those ten days alone save $20 in interest.

Now the household pays their $7,000 in expenses over the month out of the HELOC. As they do, the balance gradually rises back toward $16,000. But the average balance for the month might be around $12,000. At 8 percent, $12,000 costs about $80 in interest instead of $120. That $40 savings becomes extra principal reduction. Now add in the $2,000 surplus. That money stays in the HELOC permanently. So at the end of the month, the balance is not $18,000 anymore. It is $16,000. Next month, the same process repeats. The paycheck knocks it down, expenses raise it, but the surplus keeps locking in progress. Each month, interest gets smaller because the balance is smaller.

In about nine months, the $18,000 is gone. But now the household has a $2,000 monthly cashflow engine. They point that same system at the mortgage. They use the HELOC to push down the mortgage balance temporarily each month, crushing interest. Over time, the mortgage collapses years ahead of schedule.

Every dollar of this result comes from math, not sacrifice. The family did not earn more. They did not spend less. They simply forced money to pass through the right account at the right time. That is the power of a properly built cashflow engine.

Chapter 3

Turning Your Income Into a Debt-Destruction Machine

Most people think of income as something they earn and then spend, but in this system income is treated as a moving force. It is not the amount of money that matters most, but the way it is applied over time. When income flows through the wrong accounts, it becomes passive. When income is routed through the right structure, it becomes a machine that constantly compresses balances and erases interest. This chapter explains how to convert every paycheck, bonus, commission, and side-hustle dollar into an active weapon against debt without changing your lifestyle.

The first principle is that income must be applied immediately. When a paycheck hits a checking account and waits for bills to be paid, it is not helping you. Meanwhile, your debts are charging interest every day. By sending income directly into the revolving equity account, that money starts working against debt the moment it arrives. Even if it stays there for a few days, it creates interest savings that would never exist in a normal checking account. This is why timing matters more than amounts. A dollar applied for ten days does more than a dollar applied for one day.

The second principle is stacking. When multiple income streams arrive at different times of the month, they stack together inside the equity account, creating deeper and deeper reductions in balance. A paycheck on the first, a bonus on the fifteenth, and a side-gig payment on the twenty-second all combine to push the balance down further and further. Even though expenses will eventually pull it back up, those stacked reductions create long stretches of low balances that crush interest. Over time, this stacking effect is what creates exponential payoff instead of linear payoff.

The third principle is that expenses should never interrupt the stacking process. If expenses are paid out of checking, they force your income to leave the debt too early. When expenses are paid from the equity account, income stays applied for as long as possible. This keeps the stack intact. You want as many days as possible where multiple income deposits are sitting together against your debt, creating maximum interest suppression.

The fourth principle is prioritization. Income should always attack the most expensive debt first. That is why high-interest balances should be moved into the revolving equity account. Once they are gone, the same machine attacks the next target. Over time, your entire financial structure becomes a conveyor belt that moves money from income to high-interest debt to low-interest debt and finally into wealth.

The fifth principle is that this system rewards consistency, not perfection. You do not have to time every deposit or bill exactly. Even rough alignment creates massive benefits. As long as income enters first and expenses exit later, interest is being destroyed in between. Over months and years, that small timing difference becomes tens of thousands of dollars in savings.

By the end of this chapter, you should see income not as something you use, but as something you deploy. Every paycheck is a wave that crashes into your debt and erodes it. The more often and more deeply those waves hit, the faster the debt disappears.

Practical Example: *How Income Stacking Destroys Debt*

Imagine a household that earns $6,000 from salary on the first of the month, $2,000 from commissions on the fifteenth, and $1,000 from side work on the twenty-fifth. Their total monthly income is $9,000. Their living expenses are $6,500. They have $20,000 in high-interest debt that has been moved into a home equity line of credit at 8 percent.

On the first of the month, the $6,000 paycheck is deposited into the HELOC, dropping the balance from $20,000 to $14,000. For the next two weeks, interest is calculated on $14,000 instead of $20,000. At 8 percent, $20,000 would cost about $133 per month, or about $4.40 per day. $14,000 costs about $93 per month, or about $3.10 per day. Over fourteen days, that saves about $18 in interest.

On the fifteenth, the $2,000 commission hits and drops the balance from $14,000 to $12,000. Now interest is calculated on $12,000 instead of $20,000. That costs about $80 per month, or $2.65 per day. For the next ten days, that saves about $18 more in interest.

On the twenty-fifth, the $1,000 side income drops the balance to $11,000. That reduces daily interest to about $2.40 per day. For the last five days of the month, that saves another $10.

Meanwhile, expenses totaling $6,500 are paid throughout the month out of the HELOC. As they are paid, the balance slowly rises, but the average balance for the month might be around $13,000 instead of $20,000. At 8 percent, $13,000 costs about $87 in interest instead of $133. That $46 is extra principal reduction.

Add that to the $2,500 surplus cash flow, and now the household is effectively paying off about $2,546 per month instead of $2,500. Over a year, that extra $552 comes purely from interest collapse. As the balance drops, this effect grows stronger every month. That is how income stacking turns ordinary paychecks into a powerful debt-destruction machine.

Chapter 4

Eliminating High-Interest Debt First

High-interest debt is the single greatest enemy of financial progress because it drains cash flow faster than anything else. Credit cards, personal loans, and unsecured lines of credit often charge two to three times more interest than mortgages or home equity lines. This means that even if you are paying thousands of dollars per month, a large portion of that money is being consumed by interest instead of reducing what you owe. The Cashflow Accelerator Method always begins by eliminating these high-interest balances first because every dollar of interest you stop paying becomes new cash flow that can be used to eliminate the next debt even faster.

The reason high-interest debt must be attacked first is mathematical, not emotional. If you have a credit card at 20 percent and a mortgage at 6 percent, the credit card is costing you more than three times as much money for every dollar you owe. That means a $10,000 credit card is more dangerous to your financial future than a $30,000 mortgage balance. By moving that high-interest debt into a lower-interest revolving equity account, you immediately cut the interest rate, and then by applying income to it daily, you collapse the balance far faster than minimum payments ever could.

When high-interest debt is transferred into the revolving equity account, it stops behaving like a long-term loan and starts behaving like a flexible, shrinking target. Every paycheck that comes in temporarily pushes that balance down. Every bill that goes out slowly lets it rise again. But the average balance is always falling because surplus cash flow remains buried inside the debt. This creates a snowball effect where the interest bill shrinks every month, freeing up more and more money to apply toward principal.

Another hidden benefit of eliminating high-interest debt early is psychological. When credit cards and consumer loans disappear, your monthly obligations drop dramatically. That increases your cash flow even if your income stays the same. More cash flow means deeper balance reductions when income hits, which means faster interest destruction. The system feeds itself. The faster you remove expensive debt, the faster everything else falls.

Many people worry that using home equity to pay off credit cards is risky. In reality, it is far more dangerous to leave high-interest debt sitting where it is. A 20 percent credit card will destroy your financial future much faster than an 8 percent home equity line that is actively being paid down with cash flow. The risk comes from misuse, not from the tool itself. When equity is used as a temporary conduit for cash flow, not a permanent balance, it becomes a powerful accelerator instead of a liability.

Once the high-interest debt is gone, the same system is redirected toward the next most expensive target. This creates a waterfall where debt disappears in the order that hurts you the most. You are not guessing or hoping. You are following the math.

By the end of this chapter, you should understand that not all debt is equal. The order in which you eliminate balances determines how fast you become free. High-interest debt must go first, because it is the fastest way to increase your available cash flow and supercharge the entire system.

Practical Example: *Crushing Credit Cards First*

Let's look at a homeowner who has $12,000 in credit cards at 22 percent, $18,000 in personal loans at 14 percent, and a $250,000 mortgage at 6 percent. Their monthly income is $7,500 and their expenses including the mortgage total $6,000, leaving $1,500 in surplus cash flow. They also have a $50,000 home equity line of credit at 8 percent.

First, they use the HELOC to pay off the $12,000 credit cards and $18,000 personal loan. The HELOC balance becomes $30,000. Instead of paying 22 percent and 14 percent, they are now paying 8 percent. The credit cards alone were costing about $220 per month in interest. The personal loan was costing about $210 per month. That is $430 per month in interest. The HELOC at 8 percent on $30,000 costs about $200 per month. That immediately frees up $230 per month in cash flow.

Now their surplus is no longer $1,500. It is $1,730 because they are no longer bleeding high-interest interest. That $1,730 stays in the HELOC permanently, reducing the balance every month.

When their $7,500 paycheck is deposited into the HELOC, it drops the balance from $30,000 to $22,500. As they pay $6,000 in expenses over the month, the balance rises back to about $28,500. But because $1,730 stays behind, the balance is still shrinking.

The average balance might be around $25,000 for the month instead of $30,000. At 8 percent, $25,000 costs about $167 in interest instead of $200. That $33 savings is extra principal reduction.

So now instead of paying $1,730 toward principal, they are effectively paying $1,763. Over a year, that adds up to over $400 in extra payoff just from interest collapse.

In about 17 months, the $30,000 is gone. At that point, they have eliminated all consumer debt. Their cash flow jumps again because those minimum payments are gone. Now they might have $2,500 per month attacking the mortgage. The same engine that crushed the credit cards now crushes the house.

That is how eliminating high-interest debt first turns a slow payoff into a financial avalanche.

Chapter 5

Using Equity Without Increasing Risk

One of the biggest misunderstandings about using home equity in a debt-elimination system is the fear that borrowing against your house automatically increases danger. In reality, risk is not created by using equity; it is created by allowing balances to remain high and uncontrolled. When equity is used as a short-term transit account instead of a long-term loan, it actually reduces financial risk because it lowers total interest, improves cash flow, and shortens the amount of time any debt exists. The Cashflow Accelerator Method is designed so that equity is constantly being repaid by income, not allowed to grow unchecked.

The key to using equity safely is understanding that you are not increasing the amount of debt you have. You are repositioning it. A $20,000 credit card balance moved into a home equity line does not create new debt; it changes where the debt sits and how it behaves. The interest rate drops, and now that balance becomes exposed to your daily cash flow. Instead of being locked into a fixed payment schedule that barely touches principal, it becomes a flexible target that your income can attack every day. This makes the balance safer, not riskier, because it is shrinking faster and costing less.

Another important layer of safety is liquidity. When your money is sitting in checking or savings while you carry debt, you are actually less safe because you are paying interest unnecessarily. By keeping surplus cash inside the equity account, you are building a financial buffer. That money can be pulled back out instantly in an emergency, but while it sits there it is reducing your balance. This creates a dual-purpose safety net that both protects you and accelerates your progress.

Risk is also reduced because this system increases your margin of error. As debt disappears, your required monthly payments drop. That means you need less income to survive. If you lose a job, get sick, or face a downturn, your financial stress is lower because you have fewer obligations. Eliminating debt quickly is one of the strongest forms of financial security you can create.

The Cashflow Accelerator Method never encourages maxing out equity or chasing investments with borrowed money. It is focused on collapsing existing debt first. As balances shrink, available credit grows. That means you always have more room, not less. This rising availability is another form of safety because it means you can absorb shocks without going into crisis.

By the time you understand this chapter, you will realize that debt itself is the risk, not the tool used to eliminate it. Equity, when used as a controlled conduit for cash flow, is simply a lever that lets your income do its job faster.

Practical Example: *How Equity Use Actually Reduces Risk*

Consider a homeowner with $22,000 in credit card debt at 21 percent, a $15,000 auto loan at 9 percent, and a $280,000 mortgage at 6 percent. Their income is $8,500 per month and their expenses including debt payments total $7,200, leaving $1,300 in surplus. They have a $70,000 home equity line at 8 percent.

First, they use the HELOC to pay off the $22,000 credit cards and the $15,000 auto loan. The HELOC balance becomes $37,000. The credit cards were costing about $385 per month in interest. The auto loan was costing about $112. That is $497 per month. The HELOC at 8 percent on $37,000 costs about $247 per month. That frees up $250 in cash flow instantly.

Now their surplus is $1,550 instead of $1,300. That $1,550 stays in the HELOC every month, permanently shrinking the balance.

When their $8,500 paycheck hits the HELOC, the balance drops from $37,000 to $28,500. Over the month, $7,200 in expenses are paid out, raising it back to about $35,700. But because $1,550 stays behind, the balance still shrinks. The average balance might be around $32,000 instead of $37,000. At 8 percent, $32,000 costs about $213 in interest instead of $247. That $34 savings becomes extra principal reduction.

So instead of paying $1,550, they effectively pay $1,584 per month. Over a year, that is over $400 in additional payoff from interest collapse alone. In about 23 months, the $37,000 is gone. Now they have zero consumer debt and over $1,500 per month in free cash flow. That makes them dramatically safer than when they started.

They did not increase risk. They eliminated it.

Chapter 6

How to Turn Monthly Cash Flow Into Exponential Debt Paydown

Most people think debt is paid off in a straight line, but in reality it behaves like a curve. In the early years, interest consumes most of what you pay. In the later years, more of your payment goes toward principal. The Cashflow Accelerator Method reverses this curve by collapsing interest early, which causes principal reduction to accelerate much sooner than it normally would. When interest shrinks faster, every dollar you send works harder, and that creates exponential rather than linear progress.

Monthly cash flow is the engine that drives this process. Cash flow is what remains after all expenses are paid. In a traditional system, cash flow sits in checking or is spent, while debts continue to generate interest. In this system, cash flow is forced into the revolving equity account where it permanently reduces balances. As balances fall, interest falls. As interest falls, more cash flow becomes available. That creates a positive feedback loop where each month is more powerful than the last.

The key concept here is that interest is a moving target. You are not fighting a fixed enemy. Every time you reduce the balance, you weaken the force working against you. When you collapse interest early, you reduce the amount of time the bank has to collect it. This is why the first few months of this system are so important. Once the interest burden drops, momentum builds rapidly.

Another important factor is compounding in your favor. Normally, interest compounds against you. In this system, interest savings compound for you. Each dollar of interest you do not pay becomes extra principal reduction. That reduces the balance further, which reduces interest even more. Over time, this creates a snowball effect that speeds up payoff far beyond what minimum payments could ever achieve.

This is why people using this system often eliminate decades of debt in a fraction of the time. They are not paying more money. They are redirecting money so that interest starves and principal is constantly attacked.

By the end of this chapter, you should understand that cash flow is not just extra money. It is leverage. When applied correctly, it multiplies itself through interest reduction and creates exponential progress toward freedom.

Practical Example: *How Cash Flow Multiplies Itself*

Let's look at a household with $200,000 left on their mortgage at 6 percent and $30,000 in consumer debt moved into a HELOC at 8 percent. Their income is $7,500 per month. Their expenses including the mortgage are $6,000, leaving $1,500 in cash flow.

That $1,500 stays inside the HELOC every month. At the start, the HELOC balance is $30,000. After the first month, it drops to $28,500. At 8 percent, $30,000 costs about $200 per month in interest. $28,500 costs about $190. That $10 difference becomes extra principal reduction.

In month two, the balance drops to $26,990 instead of $27,000 because of interest savings. Each month, the interest portion shrinks, and more of the $1,500 attacks principal.

After one year, the balance is not $12,000 as it would be with straight payments. It is closer to $10,500 because interest collapsed faster. That extra $1,500 in savings came purely from the system.

Now that $1,500 in monthly cash flow is attacking the mortgage. The same interest collapse happens again. That is how exponential debt destruction works.

Chapter 7

Using the System to Eliminate Your Mortgage Decades Early

The final and most powerful stage of the Cashflow Accelerator Method begins when consumer debt is gone and the full force of your household cash flow is redirected toward your home. This is where most people experience the greatest financial transformation, because the mortgage is usually the largest and longest debt they will ever carry. A traditional thirty-year loan is designed so that you spend the first decade mostly paying interest, not principal. That means your equity grows slowly while the bank collects most of the money. The Cashflow Accelerator Method flips that equation by forcing the mortgage balance down much earlier, starving interest before it has time to accumulate.

The key to this stage is understanding that a mortgage is just another balance that responds to daily pressure. When you make one payment per month, the balance remains high for the entire month and interest is charged on the full amount. But when you use a revolving equity account as a control valve, you can temporarily suppress the mortgage balance whenever income arrives. Even if that money must be used again for expenses, the days when the balance is lower permanently reduce the total interest you will ever pay. This is what allows homeowners to collapse decades of interest without refinancing or increasing payments.

At this stage, your income becomes incredibly powerful because all high-interest debt has already been eliminated. That means every dollar of cash flow can be directed toward the mortgage. When that cash flow enters the revolving equity account, it is then applied to the mortgage, pushing the principal down far more often than once per month. This creates a constant downward pressure that accelerates payoff dramatically.

Another critical advantage here is that your cash flow grows as debts disappear. When credit cards, personal loans, and auto loans are gone, the money that used to service those debts now attacks the mortgage. That creates a compounding effect where each eliminated debt increases the power of the next stage. By the time you are focused on the mortgage, your household often has thousands of dollars per month available to apply against it, even if your income has not changed.

This stage also reduces financial risk faster than any other. A mortgage-free home means your largest expense disappears. That dramatically lowers the amount of income you need to survive. It increases your resilience against job loss, medical emergencies, and economic downturns. In many ways, paying off your mortgage early is the ultimate form of financial security.

The Cashflow Accelerator Method does not require aggressive or risky behavior to achieve this. It simply uses timing, flow, and structure to attack interest relentlessly. The earlier you begin applying this system to your mortgage, the more powerful the results become, because interest is starved before it has time to grow.

By the end of this chapter, you should see your home not as a thirty-year obligation, but as a balance that can be controlled, compressed, and eliminated far sooner than you were ever told.

Practical Example: *Collapsing a 30-Year Mortgage in a Fraction of the Time*

Let's look at a homeowner with a $300,000 mortgage at 6 percent. Their monthly payment is about $1,800. They have already eliminated all consumer debt using the Cashflow Accelerator Method. Their monthly income is $9,000 and their total living expenses excluding the mortgage are $4,200. That means they have $3,000 per month in cash flow available.

They also have a $100,000 home equity line of credit. Each month, when their $9,000 income arrives, it is deposited into the HELOC. Then $3,000 of that is immediately applied toward the mortgage principal through the HELOC, temporarily dropping the mortgage balance from $300,000 to $297,000. Over the month, the $4,200 in living expenses is paid from the HELOC, slowly raising the balance again. But the key is that for many days, the mortgage balance is far lower than it would be under the normal system.

At 6 percent, $300,000 costs about $1,500 per month in interest. If the average balance during the month is reduced to $285,000 because of income stacking, the interest is about $1,425 instead. That $75 difference becomes extra principal reduction. Add that to the $3,000 cash flow, and now the mortgage is shrinking by about $3,075 per month instead of $3,000.

Over a year, that extra $900 from interest collapse accelerates the payoff. As the balance drops, interest drops further, making the system more powerful every month. Instead of taking 30 years to pay off the home, this homeowner can eliminate the mortgage in roughly 8 to 10 years without increasing their income or lifestyle sacrifices.

That is the power of turning your cash flow into a precision tool against interest.

Chapter 8

How to Protect Your Cashflow System from Failure

The most powerful financial system in the world is useless if it is fragile. The Cashflow Accelerator Method is designed to be aggressive against debt but conservative when it comes to risk, and this chapter explains how to protect the system so that it keeps working even when life throws surprises your way. Income changes, emergencies happen, and markets fluctuate, but a properly structured cashflow system can absorb those shocks without collapsing. The goal is not just to eliminate debt, but to build a structure that is resilient, flexible, and safe.

The first layer of protection is liquidity. Many people believe that safety comes from having cash in a savings account, but when you are carrying debt, that cash is actually costing you money because it is not reducing interest. In this system, your liquidity lives inside the revolving equity account. When your surplus cash sits there, it lowers your balance and reduces interest. At the same time, it is instantly available if you need it. This creates a dual-purpose reserve that is always working for you, not sitting idle. The second layer of protection is margin. As your balances fall, your available credit increases. This gives you more room to absorb unexpected expenses. If a major repair, medical bill, or income disruption occurs, you have immediate access to funds without needing to apply for new loans. This growing margin is one of the hidden strengths of the Cashflow Accelerator Method.

The third layer is cashflow stability. As debts disappear, your monthly obligations drop. That means your lifestyle becomes easier to support. Even if your income temporarily declines, you are far less likely to fall behind. A household with no consumer debt and a shrinking mortgage is dramatically more stable than one that is buried in high-interest payments.

The fourth layer is discipline. The system works best when income flows into the equity account automatically and expenses flow out automatically. This removes emotional decision-making and prevents you from accidentally breaking the structure. The more automated the system, the safer it becomes.

The fifth layer is conservative leverage. This method never encourages maxing out equity or chasing risky investments. Its purpose is to eliminate debt and build stability. By keeping balances moving downward and available credit moving upward, you ensure that the system remains strong even in uncertain times. By now, you should understand that safety is not about avoiding all use of credit. It is about maintaining control, flexibility, and momentum so that no single event can derail your financial progress.

Practical Example: *How the System Survives a Financial Shock*

Imagine a homeowner who started with $35,000 in consumer debt and a $250,000 mortgage. After two years of using the Cashflow Accelerator Method, the consumer debt is gone and the mortgage is down to $210,000. Their income is $8,000 per month and their expenses including the mortgage are $5,500, giving them $2,500 in monthly cash flow. They also have a $90,000 home equity line, of which only $10,000 is currently used.

That means they have $80,000 of available credit sitting as a safety buffer. Their $2,500 surplus stays inside the HELOC every month, continuously reducing their balances and increasing their available credit. If nothing goes wrong, the system keeps accelerating.

Now imagine a sudden emergency: a $20,000 medical bill. Instead of panicking or taking out a high-interest loan, they simply draw $20,000 from the HELOC. Their balance rises from $10,000 to $30,000. At 8 percent, that costs about $200 per month in interest. But their $2,500 cash flow immediately starts pushing that balance back down.

Their $8,000 income hits the HELOC, dropping the balance. Their $5,500 in expenses raises it. But the $2,500 surplus stays and reduces the balance every month. In less than nine months, the $20,000 emergency is gone. During that time, the mortgage continues shrinking and interest continues collapsing.

Nothing broke. No debt spiral occurred. The system absorbed the shock and continued moving forward. That is what financial resilience looks like.

Chapter 9

How to Turn Debt Freedom Into Permanent Wealth

The ultimate goal of the Cashflow Accelerator Method is not just to get out of debt, but to transform the financial power that debt once consumed into a permanent wealth-building engine. When interest is no longer draining your income, your cash flow becomes an asset. Every dollar that used to go to banks now belongs to you. This chapter explains how to redirect that newly freed cash flow so that it builds security, income, and long-term financial independence instead of disappearing into lifestyle inflation.

The first shift that must happen after debt is eliminated is psychological. Many people unconsciously replace debt payments with spending. If a $2,000 monthly credit card and loan burden disappears, they often find new ways to use that money without realizing it. The Cashflow Accelerator Method treats that freed cash flow as sacred. It is not extra money to be consumed. It is capital to be deployed. When you maintain the same disciplined flow structure, the system that destroyed debt now begins to build wealth. The second shift is structural. The same revolving equity account that was used to suppress debt becomes a central hub for accumulating capital. Surplus cash remains inside it, reducing any remaining mortgage or sitting as available credit. Over time, this creates a large pool of deployable capital that can be used for investments, business opportunities, or passive income streams. You are no longer dependent on saving slowly. You have a financial engine that creates liquidity constantly.

The third shift is strategic. When you invest or start businesses using this system, you are not borrowing recklessly. You are using temporarily available capital that is constantly being refilled by cash flow. This allows you to pursue opportunities without destroying your stability. If an investment fails, your income continues to refill the system. If it succeeds, it accelerates your progress even more.

The fourth shift is compounding. Wealth grows the same way debt shrinks in this system: through the relentless application of cash flow. Interest no longer works against you. Returns now work for you. Over time, small monthly surpluses become large capital pools, and large capital pools become income-producing assets.

By the time you finish this chapter, you should see that debt freedom is not the end. It is the beginning of a completely different financial life.

Practical Example: *Turning $2,500 per Month Into a Wealth Engine*

Imagine a homeowner who has eliminated all consumer debt and paid their mortgage down to a small balance. They now have $2,500 per month in free cash flow that used to go to debt. Instead of spending it, they leave it inside their revolving equity account.

After one year, that $2,500 per month adds up to $30,000. But because it was sitting inside the account reducing interest, it also created thousands of dollars in interest savings. Let's say it created an additional $2,000 in reduced interest. That means their available capital is now $32,000.

They use $25,000 of that to start a small rental property investment or online business. That investment produces $500 per month in income. Now their cash flow is $3,000 per month instead of $2,500. That $3,000 stays in the system, compounding faster.

After another year, that $3,000 per month becomes $36,000 plus interest savings. Now they have over $70,000 in capital. The system snowballs, creating permanent wealth.

That is how the Cashflow Accelerator Method turns debt freedom into financial independence.

Chapter 10

Building a Lifetime Financial Control System

The Cashflow Accelerator Method is not just a way to get out of debt. It is a permanent operating system for your money. Once you understand how to control the flow of cash through your accounts, you never have to return to the old way of waiting, hoping, and reacting. This chapter explains how to lock in everything you have learned so that your finances remain optimized for the rest of your life, regardless of income changes, market cycles, or personal transitions.

The first step in building lifetime control is maintaining the flow structure. Income must always enter the revolving equity account first. Expenses must always leave it. This keeps your money working against interest at all times. Even when you are debt-free, this structure creates constant liquidity and ensures that idle cash is always reducing some balance or sitting ready for deployment.

The second step is automation. When income deposits and bill payments are automated, discipline is no longer required. The system runs on its own. This prevents you from drifting back into inefficient habits. Automation is what turns a strategy into a permanent financial machine.

The third step is scaling. As your income grows, the same structure becomes more powerful. Every raise, business profit, or investment return flows into the same engine, creating larger and faster compounding. You do not need new strategies as you become wealthier. The same system simply accelerates.

The fourth step is protection. By maintaining high available credit and low balances, you ensure that you always have a buffer against emergencies. This makes you resilient and confident, even in uncertain times.

Practical Example: A Lifetime Financial Control System

Imagine a family that now has no consumer debt and only $100,000 left on their mortgage. They earn $10,000 per month and spend $6,000. Their $4,000 surplus flows into their revolving equity account every month.

After two years, that $4,000 per month becomes $96,000 plus interest savings. Their mortgage is gone. They now have no required debt payments. Their $10,000 income is almost entirely free cash flow.

That cash flow now builds wealth. If they invest $50,000 and earn $500 per month, their system grows even faster. Over time, their financial control becomes permanent.

That is the power of building a lifetime financial system.

Chapter 11

The Exit: When and How to Fully Eliminate All Debt

The final stage of the Cashflow Accelerator Method is what turns a powerful system into permanent freedom. Up to this point, you have learned how to compress interest, accelerate cash flow, and use home equity as a control valve to destroy debt faster than traditional systems allow. Now comes the most important decision of all: when and how to fully exit debt and lock in financial independence. This stage is not about slowing down. It is about choosing the exact moment when leverage is no longer needed and converting your financial machine into a pure wealth and safety engine.

Many people make the mistake of thinking they should remain in debt forever simply because they are comfortable with the system. But debt, even when controlled, still creates exposure. The Cashflow Accelerator Method is designed to use debt as a temporary tool, not a permanent condition. The moment you reach a point where your cash flow can eliminate all remaining balances without destabilizing your life, it is time to close the loop. That is when the system delivers its final and greatest reward: full ownership of your income and your home. The exit phase begins when your mortgage balance and any remaining revolving equity balance fall below a critical threshold, usually when they are small enough that your monthly cash flow could wipe them out within one to two years. At this point, interest is already minimal. The psychological and financial benefit of being completely debt-free outweighs any minor advantage of keeping balances open. You are no longer fighting a massive interest monster. You are finishing the job.

During this stage, your cash flow should remain routed through the same structure, but now it is focused on eliminating the final balances completely. Income still flows into the revolving account. Expenses still flow out. But instead of allowing balances to float, you deliberately allow them to hit zero and stay there. This is the moment when the system flips from acceleration mode to consolidation mode.

One of the most powerful aspects of this stage is certainty. When you know that you can eliminate all debt within a short window, financial stress disappears. You are no longer reacting to bills, rates, or economic shifts. You are executing a controlled shutdown of debt. Every month, balances drop. Every month, your net worth rises. This creates a sense of control that most people never experience in their entire financial lives.

Once the last balance is paid, the revolving equity account does not disappear. It simply becomes a liquidity and opportunity engine. Your income still flows through it. Your expenses still leave it. But now, instead of reducing debt, your money accumulates as available capital. You have effectively turned your home and income into a private financial system that replaces banks, credit cards, and traditional borrowing.

By the end of this chapter, you should understand that debt freedom is not accidental. It is the result of a deliberate, structured exit that locks in everything you have built. This is where the Cashflow Accelerator Method fulfills its promise: not just faster payoff, but complete financial sovereignty.

Practical Example: *Executing the Final Exit With Real Numbers*

Let's look at a homeowner who has used the Cashflow Accelerator Method for several years. They now have only $40,000 left on their mortgage and a $10,000 balance on their home equity line. Their income is $9,000 per month and their total living expenses including housing are $5,500. That leaves $3,500 per month in cash flow.

At this stage, interest on $50,000 at an average of 7 percent is about $292 per month. That is already very low compared to where they started. Their $3,500 cash flow flows into the revolving equity account every month, reducing balances. In the first month, the $3,500 drops the combined balance from $50,000 to $46,500. Over the month, expenses of $5,500 are paid out, but because the system is structured correctly, the surplus still remains buried inside the balance.

The average balance might be around $48,000 for the month. At 7 percent, that costs about $280 in interest instead of $292. That $12 savings becomes extra principal reduction. So instead of paying down $3,500, they effectively pay $3,512.

Month after month, this continues. As the balance drops to $40,000, interest falls to about $233 per month. As it drops to $30,000, interest falls to about $175. The system accelerates as it finishes.

In about fourteen months, the full $50,000 is gone. The homeowner now owns their home free and clear and has zero debt. Their $9,000 income now flows into the equity account and builds available capital instead of fighting balances. After one year of being debt-free, they have over $40,000 in liquid capital, plus a fully paid-off home.

That is what a true financial exit looks like.

Chapter 12

Life After Debt: Turning Your Cashflow Into Legacy Wealth

Reaching the point where all debt is eliminated is one of the most powerful financial moments a person can experience, but it is also one of the most dangerous if it is not handled correctly. Without a clear plan, many people drift back into old habits, replacing debt payments with lifestyle spending. The Cashflow Accelerator Method is designed so that once debt is gone, the same system that destroyed it automatically shifts into wealth creation. This chapter explains how to keep the structure intact so that your cashflow builds security, income, and long-term family wealth for decades to come.

The first principle of life after debt is to preserve the flow. Income should still enter the revolving equity account first, even if the balance is zero. This keeps your money centralized and controlled. When income enters this account, it either reduces a balance or increases available credit. Either way, your financial power grows. Expenses still flow out of this same account, maintaining the timing advantage that made the system work in the first place. The second principle is capital accumulation. When there is no debt to reduce, surplus cash flow becomes capital. That capital is not just savings. It is deployable power. You can use it to invest, acquire assets, start businesses, or support family goals. Because it remains inside the revolving structure, it is always available and always compounding in your favor.

The third principle is income expansion. As you deploy capital into income-producing assets, your monthly cash flow increases. That increased cash flow flows right back into the same system, compounding your financial growth. What once destroyed debt now builds wealth faster and faster.

The fourth principle is generational thinking. When your home is paid off and your cashflow system is strong, you can structure your finances to benefit your children and future generations. You are no longer just surviving. You are designing a legacy.

By the end of this chapter, you should understand that freedom from debt is not the finish line. It is the starting line for a completely different financial future.

Practical Example: *From Debt-Free to Million-Dollar Net Worth*

Imagine a family that has just paid off their home and has no debt. Their income is $10,000 per month and their living expenses are $5,000. That means they have $5,000 in surplus cash flow every month. That $5,000 stays inside their revolving equity account, building capital.

After one year, that is $60,000. If interest savings add another $2,000, they now have $62,000 in deployable capital. They invest $50,000 into a rental property or business that produces $700 per month in income. Now their monthly cash flow is $5,700 instead of $5,000.

That $5,700 stays in the system. After another year, that becomes $68,400 plus interest savings. They now have over $80,000 in capital. They invest again. Each cycle increases income and capital faster.

Over ten years, this system can easily exceed $1 million in net worth, all built from cashflow and structure, not luck.

Chapter 13

How to Run This System Through Any Economy

One of the greatest strengths of the Cashflow Accelerator Method is that it is not dependent on perfect conditions. It works in strong economies, weak economies, rising rate environments, and recessions because it is built on fundamentals rather than speculation. This chapter explains how to adjust the system when interest rates rise, when income fluctuates, or when the economy slows, so that you continue to move forward no matter what happens.

The first principle of running this system in any economy is flexibility. Because your money is centralized in a revolving equity account, you can instantly change direction. If income drops, you simply slow the rate of debt reduction. If expenses rise, the system absorbs the change. You are never locked into rigid payment schedules that can break under pressure. This flexibility is what allows the system to survive and thrive when others fail.

The second principle is cashflow protection. In uncertain times, surplus cash should remain inside the revolving structure instead of being invested aggressively. That keeps your liquidity high and your risk low. Even when you pause investing, the system continues to reduce interest and build safety.

The third principle is interest management. Rising rates increase the cost of carrying debt, which makes the Cashflow Accelerator Method even more powerful. The faster you collapse balances, the less those higher rates can hurt you. This is why the system often performs better when rates rise.

The fourth principle is opportunity readiness. Economic downturns create opportunities. Because your system keeps capital liquid and available, you can act when others cannot. This is how wealth is often built during difficult times.

By the end of this chapter, you will understand that this system is not fragile. It is designed to adapt and win in any environment.

Practical Example: *Using the System During a Recession*

Imagine a homeowner who has $120,000 left on their mortgage and $15,000 in a HELOC. Their income drops from $9,000 to $7,000 during a recession. Their expenses are $5,500, leaving $1,500 in cash flow instead of $3,500.

Because the system is flexible, the $1,500 still flows into the HELOC, reducing balances. Interest is lower because balances are lower. After one year, even with reduced income, their total debt drops from $135,000 to around $115,000. They survived and progressed.

When the economy recovers, their income rises again and the system accelerates.

Chapter 14

Scaling the System Across Multiple Properties and Businesses

Once you master the Cashflow Accelerator Method for your personal home, the next level of financial growth comes from applying the same principles across multiple properties and income streams. This chapter explains how to expand the system so that it works not just for one household, but for an entire portfolio of real estate, businesses, and investments. When structured correctly, every property and every business becomes part of a single integrated cashflow engine that accelerates wealth creation.

The core principle of scaling is centralization. All income from all sources should flow into a single control account, typically backed by a large revolving equity line. This allows cash flow from one property or business to temporarily support another, maximizing interest suppression across the entire system. When one property has a surplus and another has a shortfall, the system balances itself automatically. Over time, this creates stability and efficiency that isolated accounts can never achieve.

The second principle is debt prioritization across the portfolio. Not all loans are equal. High-interest business debt, private money loans, and credit lines should be collapsed first, followed by higher-rate property loans. Lower-rate, long-term mortgages can be addressed later. This ensures that cash flow is always attacking the most expensive liabilities first, maximizing the impact of every dollar.

The third principle is capital recycling. As properties and businesses generate income, that cash flow flows into the central system and becomes available to fund new acquisitions or expansions. Instead of saving for years, you are constantly redeploying cash through the same engine that destroys interest and builds equity.

The fourth principle is risk management. Scaling does not mean recklessness. By keeping balances moving downward and available credit high, you ensure that the entire portfolio remains flexible and resilient. If one property underperforms, the system absorbs the shock without forcing a sale.

Practical Example: *A Portfolio Powered by One Cashflow Engine*

Imagine an investor who owns three rental properties. Property A produces $1,200 per month in cash flow, Property B produces $800, and Property C produces $1,000. Their total rental cash flow is $3,000. They also earn $5,000 per month from their job. Their total cash flow is $8,000.

All $8,000 flows into a central HELOC-backed account. Their total expenses and loan payments are $5,500, leaving $2,500 per month in surplus. That $2,500 reduces balances across the portfolio.

If one property needs a $15,000 roof repair, the HELOC covers it. The $2,500 cash flow pays it back in six months. Nothing breaks. The system scales and survives.

That is how multiple properties become one powerful financial engine.

Chapter 15

Teaching the System to Your Family and Locking in Generational Wealth

One of the most powerful outcomes of the Cashflow Accelerator Method is not just what it does for you, but what it can do for your family. When a system is simple, logical, and repeatable, it can be passed down across generations. This chapter explains how to teach your spouse, your children, and future heirs to run this system so that wealth is not just created, but preserved and expanded for decades.

The first step in generational success is transparency. Family members must understand how money flows through the system and why it works. This is not about secrecy or control. It is about shared financial literacy. When everyone understands that income flows into a central account, expenses flow out, and surplus stays buried in the system, they can all participate in protecting and growing it.

The second step is role assignment. Different family members can manage different parts of the system, such as tracking income, paying bills, monitoring balances, or evaluating investments. This turns financial management into a collaborative process instead of a mystery handled by one person.

The third step is continuity. By keeping the same cashflow structure across generations, you ensure that wealth is not accidentally destroyed when leadership changes. The system itself becomes the family's financial backbone.

The fourth step is education through practice. Children who grow up seeing this system in action learn more than they ever could from books. They see how money works, how interest behaves, and how discipline creates freedom.

By the end of this chapter, you will understand how to turn a personal financial system into a family legacy.

Practical Example: *A Family Wealth Engine in Action*

Imagine a family where the parents have paid off their home and have $6,000 per month in surplus cash flow. They teach their adult children how the system works. That $6,000 stays inside the revolving account, building capital.

After five years, that is $360,000 plus interest savings. The family uses $200,000 to help one child start a business that generates $3,000 per month. That income flows back into the system, increasing the family's cash flow to $9,000 per month. Now the system grows even faster, benefiting multiple generations

Final Thoughts

The Cashflow Accelerator Method

Most people spend their entire financial lives chasing payments, hoping that someday their debts will simply disappear. They are told to budget harder, earn more, or wait patiently as amortization slowly does its work. But as you now understand, debt does not disappear on its own. It only shrinks when interest is starved and cash flow is allowed to attack balances continuously. That is the real breakthrough behind the Cashflow Accelerator Method. It does not rely on motivation, luck, or timing. It relies on structure, flow, and mathematics.

What you have learned in this book is not just a way to pay off debt faster. You have learned how to control money. You have learned how to turn your income into an active force instead of a passive paycheck. You have learned how to make interest work for you instead of against you. These are not tricks. They are laws of financial physics. When money flows into the right place at the right time, it changes everything.

The true power of this system is that it does not require a perfect life. You do not need to earn more. You do not need to live on rice and beans. You do not need to refinance, move, or take risks. You simply need to route the money you already earn through a better system. That is why this method works for teachers, business owners, self-employed professionals, investors, and families alike. It adapts to your life instead of forcing you to adapt to it.

As a licensed mortgage broker, I have watched countless homeowners struggle for decades because no one ever showed them how debt really behaves. I have also watched ordinary families use these same principles to erase hundreds of thousands of dollars in interest and reclaim their future. The difference was never income. It was knowledge and structure.

This book is not the end of your journey. It is the moment when you step into control. Whether you choose to become debt-free in five years, ten years, or simply build an unbreakable financial system that works quietly in the background, you now have the tools to do it with confidence.

Your home is no longer just a place to live. Your income is no longer just a paycheck. Together, they form a powerful financial engine that can fund your life, protect your family, and build a legacy.

That is what true financial freedom looks like.

How to Get a Personalized HELOC Review

If you found *HELOC Fundamentals: How Home Equity Lines of Credit Really Work — and How to Use Them Safely* helpful, you may want to see how these concepts apply to your own home, credit profile, and financial goals.

Every homeowner's situation is unique. Home value, mortgage balance, credit history, income type, and state-specific lending rules all affect how much equity you can access, what type of HELOC you may qualify for, and what terms may be available. The examples in this book are designed to teach how HELOCs work — but your real options can only be determined by reviewing your actual numbers.

If you would like a **no-obligation Home Equity Line of Credit review**, you can request one here:

Website:https://www.nodocsheloc.com

Email:info@FinibiMortgage.com

A licensed mortgage broker will review your information and explain what HELOC and home equity options may be available to you based on your specific situation.

No cost. No pressure. No obligation.

Joseph G. Correa

About the Author

Joseph G. Correa is a licensed mortgage broker and the founder of Finibi Mortgage, a Florida-based brokerage specializing in home equity, real estate investment financing, and alternative lending strategies for homeowners, business owners, and investors. With more than two decades of experience in mortgage lending, underwriting, and financial structuring, Joseph has helped thousands of borrowers access capital using intelligent, low-risk leverage rather than high-interest consumer debt.

Unlike traditional loan officers who focus only on closing transactions, Joseph's approach is rooted in long-term financial strategy. He believes that mortgages, HELOCs, and credit lines should be used as tools for building wealth, protecting cash flow, and creating financial resilience — not as traps that keep families locked into decades of unnecessary interest payments. This philosophy has made him a trusted advisor for entrepreneurs, real estate investors, and self-employed borrowers who need flexible, modern financing solutions that banks often fail to provide.

Joseph is widely known for his expertise in home equity lines of credit, no-documentation and bank-statement loan programs, investor financing, and creative equity-based strategies such as debt-elimination systems and capital recycling. His ability to translate complex lending rules into simple, actionable guidance has helped homeowners turn idle equity into productive capital for investments, businesses, and passive income.

Through his education platform, Finibi Academy, Joseph has trained tens of thousands of students worldwide in credit, mortgage strategy, real estate financing, and financial independence. His courses and books are used by first-time homeowners, seasoned investors, and financial professionals seeking a clearer, more honest understanding of how modern lending really works.

Joseph created *The Home Equity Wealth Series* to give everyday homeowners the same financial knowledge that banks, hedge funds, and institutional investors use to control capital and minimize risk. His mission is simple: to help people stop guessing, stop fearing debt, and start using smart leverage to build real financial freedom.

When he is not structuring loans or writing, Joseph works with families and investors across the United States to design personalized equity strategies that align with their goals, cash flow, and long-term wealth plans.

The Home Equity Wealth Series Roadmap

The Professional Guide to Using Your Home to Build Financial Freedom

The purpose of *The Home Equity Wealth Series* is to give homeowners the same financial tools and strategies used by banks, investors, and institutions—translated into clear, practical guidance for everyday people. Each book builds on the last, taking you from basic understanding to advanced mastery of how to use home equity safely, intelligently, and profitably across every stage of life.

Book 1 — *HELOC Fundamentals*This book gives you the foundation. You will understand how Home Equity Lines of Credit work, how they are structured, how risk is controlled, and how equity becomes usable capital. The books that follow are designed to help you apply that knowledge to your own situation, your income type, your credit profile, and your long-term financial goals.

Book 2 — *How to Qualify for a HELOC* This book shows you how lenders actually evaluate borrowers. You will learn how credit scores, income, property type, and debt ratios affect approval, limits, and interest rates. You will also learn how to position yourself to qualify for the largest possible credit line at the best possible terms.

Book 3 — *HELOCs for Real Estate Investors* This book focuses on using home equity to buy, rehab, refinance, and scale rental properties. It explains how investors use HELOCs for down payments, renovations, and portfolio growth while keeping cash flow positive and risk controlled.

Book 4 — *Self-Employed HELOC Strategies* Designed for business owners, freelancers, 1099 borrowers, and LLCs, this book explains how bank-statement income, business income, and alternative documentation can be used to qualify for home equity even when traditional tax returns do not reflect true cash flow.

Book 5 — *Credit Mastery for HELOC Approval* This book dives deep into credit strategy. You will learn how utilization, credit mix, and reporting behavior affect HELOC limits and pricing—and how to optimize your credit profile specifically for home equity approval.

Book 6 — *No-Doc & Alternative HELOC Programs* This book covers asset-based HELOCs, no-income-verification options, and non-traditional lending programs for high-net-worth, self-employed, or cash-heavy borrowers who do not fit inside standard underwriting models.

Book 7 — *Using a HELOC to Eliminate Debt* This book teaches how to use home equity to replace high-interest credit cards, personal loans, and auto loans with low-interest revolving credit, allowing borrowers to eliminate debt years faster and save tens of thousands of dollars in interest.

Book 8 — *Using a HELOC to Build Wealth* This book shows how homeowners fund investments, businesses, and passive income streams using HELOCs while maintaining liquidity and controlling risk.

Book 9 — *HELOC Risk Management* This book focuses entirely on safety. You will learn how to structure buffers, cash-flow coverage, rate protection, and leverage limits so your home becomes safer over time—not more vulnerable.

Book 10 — *The Smart Borrower's Home Equity Blueprint* The final book ties everything together into a complete lifetime strategy for using home equity as a personal banking system, investment engine, and financial safety net.

Book 11 — *The Cashflow Accelerator Method*

The Cashflow Accelerator Method is the final transformation stage of *The Home Equity Wealth Series.* While the earlier books teach how to access, qualify for, and safely use home equity, this book teaches how to **weaponize cash flow itself** to permanently eliminate debt and create lasting wealth. Together, these books are designed to turn a single asset—your home—into a lifelong financial advantage. Each volume adds another layer of understanding, allowing you to move from homeowner to capital manager, from borrower to strategist, and from financial stress to long-term stability.

This is not about taking more risk.It is about learning how money really works—and using that knowledge to build financial freedom that lasts.

Educational & Financial Disclaimer

This book is provided for **educational and informational purposes only**. The author and publisher are not engaged in rendering legal, tax, accounting, investment, or financial advice. Although the author is a licensed mortgage broker, the information in this book is intended to provide general education about Home Equity Lines of Credit (HELOCs) and home equity strategy, not personalized financial, legal, or lending advice.

Mortgage programs, underwriting guidelines, interest rates, credit requirements, and home equity products vary by lender, investor, state, and economic conditions, and may change at any time without notice. The examples, calculations, and scenarios presented in this book are hypothetical and are for illustration only. They do not represent guaranteed outcomes or actual loan approvals.

Before making any financial decisions, including applying for a HELOC, refinancing, borrowing against home equity, or using credit for investment or debt repayment, readers should consult with a qualified mortgage professional, financial advisor, tax advisor, or attorney who can evaluate their specific situation.

Risk Disclosure

Borrowing against home equity involves risk. A HELOC is secured by your home, which means failure to make required payments could result in foreclosure or loss of property. This book teaches responsible, conservative, and structured use of home equity, but no financial strategy is risk-free.

Readers are solely responsible for their financial decisions. Neither the author nor the publisher makes any warranties, express or implied, about the accuracy, completeness, or applicability of the information in this book to any individual or situation.

www.ingramcontent.com/pod-product-compliance
Ingram Content Group UK Ltd.
Pitfield, Milton Keynes, MK11 3LW, UK
UKHW020156290926
15471UKWH00005B/903

9 798295 580802